THE OFFICIAL
SHEFFIELD
UNITED FC
ANNUAL 2011

Written by Andy Pack,
Kevin Cookson and Mark Woollas

A Grange Publication

© 2010. Published by Grange Communications Ltd., Edinburgh under licence from Sheffield United Football Club. Printed in the EU.

Photographs © Press Association Images & Blades Sports Photography.

ISBN: 978-1-907104-74-9

£7.99

CONTENTS

SHEFFIELD UNITED F.C.
1889

The 2009-10 season was an eventful campaign at Bramall Lane, there's little doubt about that! Countless injuries, regular incomings and outgoings, which included a record amount of loan players, did not stop United being in the hunt for the play-offs for the majority of the season. Here's a reminder of the last campaign, see if the following pages jog your memory about your favourite moments...

AUGUST

Middlesbrough 0 Blades 0
Blades 1 Port Vale 2 – Carling Cup
(Sharp)
Blades 2 Watford 0
(Ward, Evans)
Blades 1 Leicester City 1
(Treacy)
Reading 1 Blades 3
(Quinn, Ward, Cotterill)
Blades 2 West Brom 2
(Evans, Cotterill)

Travelling to one of the newly-relegated teams, earning a deserved point and keeping a clean sheet was certainly a positive way to kick-off the campaign.

Following a difficult summer, which included losing the play-offs at the final hurdle, the Paddy Kenny situation and Tottenham's quest for the two Kyles (Walker and Naughton), Kevin Blackwell had a rebuilding exercise to complete.

This was clear in his team for the season-opener at Middlesbrough, where five players were handed their debuts – including goalkeeper, Mark Bunn, who had been brought in less than a week earlier.

The draw at the Riverside was followed by a disappointing home Carling Cup exit at the hands of Port Vale, when the resting of several first-choices still couldn't explain away the loss. The first win of the season was secured with an impressive performance against Watford when Ched Evans contributed with his first goal for the Club. Home draws with Leicester and West Brom – both of whom were starting out on successful seasons – were posted either side of a fine win at Reading who took the lead but were then stunned by impressive strikes from Quinn, Ward and Cotterill. Unbeaten at home and with three crowds around the 25,000 mark, the Blades finished August in a promising seventh place having laid the platform for another promotion assault.

SEPTEMBER

September's first day saw United bring in James Harper and Jordan Stewart along with a number of departures before the transfer deadline.

Due to an international round of fixtures it was almost a fortnight before they were given the chance to make their debuts and Harper went straight into the team for the short trip to Derby where Matt Kilgallon put pressure on Rob Hulse to score an own goal that helped the Blades up to fifth position.

The disappointment of a 3-2 defeat at Coventry was soon forgotten by an explosive Friday night in which the blue half of the Steel City was blown away inside the first half, despite the Blades having to throw loanee Andrew Davies straight into the mix after signing just hours before kick-off.

The Owls fans at the Bramall Lane end of the ground were in prime position to see Jamie Ward, then Darius Henderson and an own goal from Lewis Buxton give the Blades a 3-0 half-time advantage. Wednesday fought back after the interval and two goals added nervousness but United held on to secure bragging rights for the next seven months.

Two sendings off, a penalty and a disallowed goal in an incident-packed game followed at Swansea's Liberty Stadium but it was no consolation to Blades fans who witnessed a 2-1 defeat. The month ended with an exciting game in front of another bumper Lane crowd. Ipswich, chasing their first win of the season, held a 3-1 lead going into the last 15 minutes but late goals from Darius Henderson and Chris Morgan earned a share of the spoils.

Derby County 0 Blades 1
(own goal)
Coventry City 3 Blades 2
(Ward, Harper)
Blades 3 Sheffield Wednesday 2
(Ward, Henderson, own goal)
Swansea City 2 Blades 1
(Quinn)
Blades 3 Ipswich Town 3
(Henderson 2, Morgan)

OCTOBER

The signing of striker Richard Cresswell was not immediately popular due to his links with Sheffield Wednesday and Leeds United, but he went some way to winning over the doubters with his first goal for the club.

He grabbed United's leveller in the derby draw with Doncaster Rovers, throwing himself at the ball and the back post to score. He needed treatment for what was to prove to be cracked ribs, thus handing boss Blackwell further injury worries.

Cresswell was ruled out for a period, as were others, such as Montgomery, Ward, Davies and Treacy, although Williamson was called upon for the first time after suffering a back problem days after his summer switch from Watford. Conceding three goals twice in two away games in the space of three days – at

Scunthorpe and Blackpool – were amongst the lowlights of the season as well as the month, whilst there was also another defeat before October was completed.

However, United played their part in an entertaining seven-goal thriller against Cardiff. Darius Henderson scored twice, James Harper netted in injury-time and then Stephen Quinn had a late, late effort dubiously ruled out for offside, which would have made it 4-4! The disappointing month – both off and on the field – ended with the squad slipping from 6th to 13th in the table.

Blades 1 Doncaster Rovers 1
(Cresswell)
Scunthorpe United 3 Blades 1
(Evans)
Blackpool 3 Blades 0
Blades 3 Cardiff City 4
(Henderson 2, Harper)

NOVEMBER

The month kicked off with another defeat – although there were positives in the narrow 1-0 reversal to title-challenging Newcastle, who were reliant on their goalkeeper and a deflected goal to earn the points at the Lane. It was Darius Henderson who was denied by a last-gasp Steve Harper save in the game against the Magpies but the Blades striker was about to hit a purple patch.

Donning the captain's armband in the absence of suspended skipper Chris Morgan, Henderson held his nerve to score two penalties that earned the Blades a point in the televised derby at Barnsley.

Henderson missed the next game, a narrow home victory over Peterborough when Henri Camara scored his first goal for the club on his full debut and the recalled Mark Bunn saved a penalty. But the powerful striker did return with maximum effect for the trip to Bristol City at the end of the month.

Blades 0 Newcastle United 1
Barnsley 2 Blades 2
(Henderson 2)
Blades 1 Peterborough United 0
(Camara)
Bristol City 2 Blades 3
(Henderson 3)

United gave a debut to new loan goalkeeper Carl Ikeme and he was impressive on his bow, although it was Henderson who grabbed the headlines with all three goals in a 3-2 win. It looked like Alvaro Saborio's goal five minutes into injury-time had earned City a 2-2 draw but United went back up the field and after Kyel Reid's shot was blocked, in-form Henderson was ideally placed to net his first senior treble and help the Blades to keep in touch with the top ten in the Championship.

DECEMBER

Plymouth Argyle 0 Blades 1
(Harper)
Blades 0 Nottingham Forest 0
Blades 2 Crystal Palace 0
(Williamson, Quinn)
QPR 1 Blades 1
(Cresswell)
Leicester City 2 Blades 1
(Camara)
Blades 1 Preston NE 0
(Ward)

December kicked off in the cold and wet surroundings of Plymouth – a venue where a week earlier Barnsley's game had been abandoned because of heavy rain.

The conditions were a factor in a difficult game but it was the travelling fans who were celebrating at the death. James Harper was credited with the late goal although debutant loanee Toni Kallio may have added a vital deflection to beat the Argyle rearguard in a crowded penalty area.

Three days after the tiring trip United held an in-form Nottingham Forest, who were indebted to goalkeeper, Lee Camp, for making a string of impressive saves.

The return of Neil Warnock with his Crystal Palace team raised interest and a goal in each half from Stephen Quinn and Lee Williamson secured a victory for Blackwell against his old boss. United's final match before Christmas was in freezing conditions at QPR although a goal for each side in the first ten minutes did fend off the cold somewhat. A thunderbolt from former Blade Mikele Leigertwood gave the home side the lead but United were soon level, with Richard Cresswell benefiting from good work by Kallio, to stretch an unbeaten run to seven games.

At Leicester on Boxing Day, United had the chance to climb back into the top six but an impressive second half showing fell short of clawing back a 2-0 first-half deficit, although Henri Camara was on target soon after making an appearance as a half-time substitute.

United did, however, end 2009 with a victory. Geary completed his first 90 minutes in almost 18 months but it was another of the club's little brigade, Jamie Ward, who decided the fixture against Preston when his 35-yard curling free-kick evaded both attackers and defenders to sneak in at the far post. At the turn of the year United occupied seventh position – just two points away from a coveted top six position.

JANUARY

Richard Cresswell's reputation with Unitedites grew considerably in the early weeks, thanks to goals in four of January's six games. His personal purple patch against QPR continued, scoring the goal that secured a 1-1 third round FA Cup draw at Bramall Lane and then being influential in the replay win at Loftus Road, where Jamie Ward scored with his first touch and set up Cresswell with his second! Cresswell then scored the goal that secured a deserved home success over Middlesbrough – stooping to convert Andy Taylor's cross – whilst he was rested for the fourth round FA Cup tie at Bolton, where the Premiership side progressed.

Back in the league, United moved into the top six thanks to a 3-0 home success over Reading, where Mark Yeates made his bow.

Jonathan Fortune netted on his home debut, Cresswell continued his rich vein and Chris Morgan was also on target, whilst Mark Bunn was called upon to make a string of fine saves, including one from the penalty spot.

However, January ended with a defeat when a dodgy penalty award handed West Brom the advantage whilst a deflected goal also helped as United slipped to a 3-1 defeat.

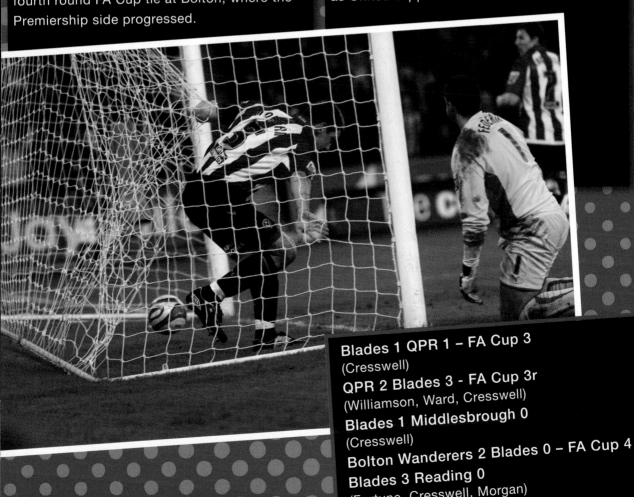

Blades 1 QPR 1 – FA Cup 3
(Cresswell)
QPR 2 Blades 3 - FA Cup 3r
(Williamson, Ward, Cresswell)
Blades 1 Middlesbrough 0
(Cresswell)
Bolton Wanderers 2 Blades 0 – FA Cup 4
Blades 3 Reading 0
(Fortune, Cresswell, Morgan)
West Brom 3 Blades 1
(Henderson)

FEBRUARY

Watford 3 Blades 0
Blades 1 Derby County 1
(Williamson)
Preston NE 2 Blades 1
(Yeates)
Blades 2 Bristol City 0
Nottingham Forest 1 Blades 0
Blades 4 Plymouth Argyle 3
(Camara, Ward 2, Cresswell)

On the first day of the month - transfer deadline day - United were rocked as the coach pulled out of Bramall Lane heading for Watford as Spurs got in contact to recall Kyle Walker.

The young defender had been in fine form in the first half of the campaign but he had to watch from the sidelines at Vicarage Road as a makeshift defence, which included Nyron Nosworthy making his debut and Chris Morgan limping off in the first half, were put under the cosh as Watford recorded a 3-0 win.

Back at the Lane, United conceded a home league goal for the first time in 592 minutes as Robbie Savage gave Derby the lead but Lee Williamson's injury-time leveller against his hometown club secured a point.

A narrow reversal at Preston, where Kyle Bartley made his debut and Mark Yeates netted his first Blades goal, followed before United secured a first win in five games at home to Bristol City, where Henri Camara and Darius Henderson were the goalscorers.

Controversy reigned during an away fixture at Nottingham Forest, when Henderson was shown a red card for an off the ball incident but United remained in contention for a top six spot with a victory in February's final fixture.

Jamie Ward netted twice in a 4-3 home victory over Plymouth Argyle but the headlines were about Richard Cresswell's cheeky goal, when he sneaked from behind goalkeeper David Stockdale before slotting into an unguarded net.

MARCH

The new manager thing came into play in March's first game – the long trip to Selhurst Park – where Paul Hart prodded a reaction from his Crystal Palace players, particularly goalkeeper Julian Speroni, who kept United at bay.

The re-arranged trip to Peterborough just three days later was one of the season's low points as the winless away run continued and the Blades picked up more injuries, this time Ched Evans and Jamie Ward were forced out of the action.

Richard Cresswell's hoodoo over QPR enabled United to avoid defeat to Neil Warnock's new charges whilst the highlight of March was the emphatic victory over fellow play-off chasers, Blackpool.

Crystal Palace 1 Blades 0
Peterborough United 1 Blades 0
Blades 1 QPR 1
(Cresswell)
Blades 3 Blackpool 0
(Cresswell 2, Montgomery)
Doncaster Rovers 1 Blades 1
(Harper)
Cardiff City 1 Blades 1
(Quinn)
Blades 0 Scunthorpe United 1

Another new face, this time Paul Connolly, was brought in on the day of the fixture against the Seasiders and he contributed to a clean sheet, whilst at the other end two more from Cresswell and a rare strike from Nick Montgomery helped the Blades back up to seventh in the table, jumping above Blackpool.

Plans for the next game, at local rivals Doncaster, were disrupted by Blackburn's recall of goalkeeper Mark Bunn and Kevin Blackwell moved instantly to secure the services of Steve Simonsen to take over in goal. The Blades recovered from conceding an early goal to pick up a point, thanks to James Harper's late finish.

A long midweek trip to Cardiff followed with Blackwell's squad again decimated through injury. Home grown Matt Lowton made his debut as a late substitute and protected a point with a clearance after Stephen Quinn's second half goal.

However, the efforts in South Wales were spoiled by a home defeat in the next game – against bogey team Scunthorpe – when a deflected goal decided the Sunday lunchtime encounter.

APRIL / MAY

Easter kicked off with a home derby although Barnsley were happy to block out United's attacking attempts, whilst Paul Connolly's sending-off caused further difficulties in team selection matters.

Connolly was unavailable for the Easter Monday trip to Newcastle, who had secured the Championship title before kick-off and there was a carnival atmosphere at St James' Park. Richard Cresswell's goal, which appeared to hit Darius Henderson on the way over the line, threatened to spoil the party but the home side hit back with a goal in each half.

The home victory over Coventry in the next game – thanks to another Cresswell goal – was deserved and boosted confidence ahead of the short trip across the city to meet old rivals Sheffield Wednesday, who were desperate for the points in their bid to avoid relegation.

Wednesday took advantage of Cresswell being off the field receiving treatment to grab the lead but Lee Williamson's free-kick denied the Owls a victory and valuable points.

United, now out of the play-off reckoning due to results elsewhere, made a severe dent in Swansea's promotion hopes with a 2-0 victory in the final home game of the season, a fixture remembered for Paddy Kenny and Gary Naysmith's first appearances of the season. The Blades rounded off the campaign with a first win at Portman Road in 35 years to secure eighth place in the Championship.

Blades 0 Barnsley 0
Newcastle United 2 Blades 1
(Cresswell)
Blades 1 Coventry City 0
Sheffield Wednesday 1 Blades 1
(Williamson)
Blades 2 Swansea City 0
(Cresswell, own goal)
Ipswich Town 0 Blades 3
(Yeates, Evans, Cresswell)

FINAL STANDINGS

Football League Championship Table 2009/10

	P	HW	HD	HL	HGF	HGA	AW	AD	AL	AGF	AGA	PTS	GD
Newcastle United	46	18	5	0	56	13	12	7	4	34	22	102	+55
West Bromwich Albion	46	16	3	4	48	21	10	10	3	41	27	91	+41
Nottingham Forest	46	18	2	3	45	13	4	11	8	20	27	79	+25
Cardiff City	46	12	6	5	37	20	10	4	9	36	34	76	+19
Leicester City	46	13	6	4	40	18	8	7	8	21	27	76	+16
Blackpool	46	13	6	4	46	22	6	7	10	28	36	70	+16
Swansea City	46	10	10	3	21	12	7	8	8	19	25	69	+3
Sheffield United	46	12	8	3	37	20	5	6	12	25	35	65	+7
Reading	46	10	7	6	39	22	7	5	11	29	41	63	+5
Bristol City	46	10	10	3	38	34	5	8	10	18	31	63	-9
Middlesbrough	46	9	8	6	25	21	7	6	10	33	29	62	+8
Doncaster Rovers	46	9	7	7	32	29	6	8	9	27	29	60	+1
Queens Park Rangers	46	8	9	6	36	28	6	6	11	22	37	57	-7
Derby Town	46	12	3	8	37	32	3	8	12	16	31	56	-10
Ipswich Town	46	8	11	4	24	23	4	9	10	26	38	56	-11
Watford	46	10	6	7	36	26	4	6	13	25	42	54	-7
Preston North End	46	9	10	4	35	26	4	5	14	23	47	54	-15
Barnsley	46	8	7	8	25	29	6	5	12	28	40	54	-16
Coventry City	46	8	9	6	27	29	5	6	12	20	35	54	-17
Scunthorpe United	46	10	7	6	40	32	4	3	16	22	52	52	-22
Crystal Palace	46	8	5	10	24	27	6	12	5	26	26	49	-3
Sheffield Wednesday	46	8	6	9	30	31	3	8	12	19	38	47	-20
Plymouth Argyle	46	5	6	12	20	30	6	2	15	23	38	41	-25
Peterborough United	46	6	5	12	32	37	2	5	16	14	43	34	-34

THE CRESSY
COLLECTION

The capture of Richard Cresswell in September 2009 was a masterstroke as the strike ace went on to claim the tag of top goalscorer last season.

Initially brought in on loan, he joined on a permanent basis in January and then signed a new three-year contract in the summer. He cracked ribs scoring his first for the club but from then on the pain turned to pleasure as 'Cressy' banged in the goals from all angles, although goalkeeper David Stockdale might not want to be reminded! Here's a rundown of the 14 goals that took him to the top of United's scoring charts for the 2009-10 campaign.

1 v Doncaster Rovers (H) 1-1

Despite being an ex-Leeds and Wednesday player, Richard went a long way to proving that he was now a Blade by throwing himself at a cross to score in a South Yorkshire derby. He collided with a post in front of the Kop but earned the Blades a point. He played out the final 25 minutes but was soon diagnosed with cracked ribs.

2 v QPR (A)   1-1

After an injury lay-off, Richard returned ahead of the hectic Christmas period and began his spell as QPR's bogeyman. The home side went ahead really early in the game but it did not take long for the equaliser to arrive when 'Cressy' got in ahead of his marker to poke home a Toni Kallio cross at the near post.

3 v QPR (H) FA Cup   1-1

When the Blades drew QPR in the FA Cup, the London side must have been wary of Richard and they were right to be - but still could not stop him scoring! Trailing again, the Blades hit back just before half-time when Cressy's header from Stephen Quinn's cross flew past Radek Cerny and into the top corner.

4 v QPR (A) FA Cup   3-2

For the third time, QPR felt his force… this time helping the Blades to progress to the fourth round of the FA Cup in the process. With a deceiving looping effort, following Jamie Ward's cross, Richard's goal was United's third of the match and put the game out of the reach of the home side.

5 v Middlesbrough (H)   1-0

The second half goal was enough to secure three more points although initially he didn't even realise he had scored. Andy Taylor and Ched Evans had linked up on the left and Richard got in ahead of David Wheater to clip the ball goalwards and when he looked back he noticed that the header had beaten Danny Coyne.

6 v Reading (H) 3-0

His header in this fixture in late January was one of the easiest of the season. With United leading 1-0 and moments after a penalty save by Mark Bunn, Kyle Walker powered down the right flank and although he was denied a goal by Adam Federici's parry, Richard was ideally placed to nod the ball into the unguarded net.

7 v Plymouth Argyle (H)   4-3

This effort made the headlines and embarrassed Plymouth goalkeeper David Stockdale. In an entertaining 4-3 win, Richard's goal after 80 minutes proved to be the winner. With the keeper getting the ball ready to clear, he was unaware that Cressy was prowling behind him and the striker stole possession before sliding it into the empty net.

THE CRESSY
COLLECTION

8 v QPR (H)   1-1

This goal is one that 'Cressy' will argue was one of his best – again against QPR! Mark Yeates caused problems down the left and although his cross was a little behind Richard, he used all his experience to angle his body and beat Carl Ikeme with another header into the top corner. It was his fourth goal in as many games against the Loftus Road club!

9 & 10 v Blackpool (H)   3-0

Good friend Nick Montgomery may have got the headlines with a rare goal but Richard set the ball rolling in the very first minute, converting a corner at the back post against the odds and then, in the second half, pushing the ball over the line from just a yard out following Darius Henderson's drilled delivery across the box.

11 v Newcastle United (A)   1-2

A contentious goal, in front of the Sky cameras, but one that has gone down in the records with Richard's name beside it. He rose highest from a left-wing corner to head United into the lead at Newcastle, although the replays may have suggested that the ball touched Darius Henderson on the way to beat Magpies' goalkeeper Steve Harper.

12 v Coventry City (H)   1-0

Another to fly into the top corner giving the goalkeeper little chance! This time it was Keiren Westwood who was beaten as 'Cressy' fired home after a neat move down the right flank that involved himself, Glen Little, Nick Montgomery and Chris Morgan. Again it proved to be the only goal of the game - and a winner.

13 v Swansea City (H)   2-0

He added another one against Swansea in the final home game and if he had his own way it would have been two! Just after the hour, a deflected cross from Mark Yeates saw 'Cressy' react well and fire home a half-volley and then late on he took the plaudits for his role in United's second, which went down as an own goal off goalkeeper Dorus de Vries.

14 v Ipswich Town (A) 3-0

Fitting that the club's leading goalscorer claimed the final goal of the season! The points were already in the bag before Mark Yeates saw his shot parried by Ipswich goalkeeper Brian Murphy and 'Cressy' rounded off the campaign with a rebound header that managed to find the back of the net with the aid of the crossbar.

1. STEVE SIMONSEN
DoB: 3.4.79, South Shields
Height: 6ft 1ins, Weight: 14st 13lbs
Signed from: Stoke City
Previous clubs: Stoke City, Everton, Tranmere Rovers
FACT SLOT: One of Steve's middle names is Preben and he supported Sunderland as a boy.

2. STEPHEN JORDAN
DoB: 6.3.82, Warrington
Height: 6ft 0ins, Weight: 12st 6lbs
Signed from: Burnley
Previous clubs: Burnley, Cambridge United (loan), Manchester City
FACT SLOT: Kevin Keegan and Stuart Pearce were amongst the managers Stephen had at Manchester City.

3. NYRON NOSWORTHY
DoB: 11.10.80, Brixton
Height: 6ft 0ins, Weight: 14st 11lbs
Signed from: Sunderland (loan)
Previous clubs: Sunderland, Gillingham
FACT SLOT: Nyron's nickname is Nugsy, given to him by his parents when he was young.

4. NICK MONTGOMERY
DoB: 28.10.81, Leeds
Height: 5ft 10ins, Weight: 12st 11lbs
Signed from: Youth team
Previous clubs: None
FACT SLOT: Nick has played for Scotland at U21s level, despite being a born and bred Yorkshireman.

5. CHRIS MORGAN
DoB: 9.11.77, Barnsley
Height: 6ft 0ins, Weight: 13st 11lbs
Signed from: Barnsley
Previous clubs: Barnsley
FACT SLOT: Don't shout it too loud, but Chris has been sent off for the Blades more times than any other player.

6. JOHNNY ERTL
DoB: 13.11.82, Graz, Austria
Height: 6ft 2ins, Weight: 13st 3lbs
Signed from: Crystal Palace
Previous clubs: Crystal Palace, Austria Vienna, SC Kalsdorf (loan), Sturm Graz
FACT SLOT: Austrian international Johnny's real name is Johannes but prefers to be called Johnny.

7. DARIUS HENDERSON
DoB: 7.9.81, Sutton
Height: 6ft 2ins, Weight: 14st 7lbs
Signed from: Watford
Previous clubs: Watford, Swindon Town (loan), Gillingham, Brighton (loan), Reading
FACT SLOT: The hat-trick Darius scored against Bristol City last season was his first treble at senior level.

8. LEON BRITTON
DoB: 16.9.82, Wandsworth
Height: 5ft 4ins, Weight: 10st 1lbs
Signed from: Swansea City
Previous clubs: Swansea City, West Ham.
FACT SLOT: Leon wanted the number 7 shirt when he signed for United but had to settle for 8.

9. CHED EVANS
DoB: 28.12.88, St Asaph, Wales
Height: 5ft 11ins, Weight: 13st 5lbs
Signed from: Manchester City
Previous clubs: Norwich City (loan), Manchester City
FACT SLOT: Ched scored the winner, with a back heel, on his full debut for Wales.

10. DANIEL BOGDANOVIC
DoB: 26.3.80, Misurata, Libya
Height: 6ft 1ins, Weight: 12st 1lbs
Signed from: Barnsley
Previous clubs: Barnsley, Lokomotiv Sofia, Cisco Roma, Marsaxlokk, Sliema Wanderers, Cherno More, Valletta, Naxxar Lions, Vasas
FACT SLOT: Before arriving in England, the Maltese international had played in Italy, Bulgaria and Hungary.

11. MARK YEATES
DoB: 11.1.85, Tallaght, Ireland
Height: 5ft 8ins, Weight: 10st 8lbs
Signed from: Middlesbrough
Previous clubs: Middlesbrough, Colchester United, Leicester City (loan), Hull City (loan), Swindon Town (loan), Brighton (loan), Tottenham Hotspur
FACT SLOT: Kevin Blackwell wanted to sign Mark before he signed for Middlesbrough but had to wait another six months to get his man.

13. MIHKEL AKSALU
DoB: 7.11.84, Kuressaare, Estonia
Height: 6ft 4ins, Weight: 13st 4lbs
Signed from: Flora Tallinn
Previous clubs: Flora Tallin, Tervis Parnu, HUJK Emmaste, Sorve JK, Muhumaa JK, FC Kuressaare
FACT SLOT: Mihkel was named the Baltic League's Goalkeeper of the Year in 2007.

14. LEE WILLIAMSON
DoB: 7.6.82, Derby
Height: 5ft 11ins, Weight: 12st 6lbs
Signed from: Watford
Previous clubs: Watford, Preston North End (loan), Rotherham United, Northampton Town, Mansfield Town
FACT SLOT: Despite being from Derby, he is eligible to play for Jamaica.

15. RYAN FRANCE
DoB: 13.12.80, Sheffield
Height: 5ft 11ins, Weight: 12st 2lbs
Signed from: Hull City
Previous clubs: Hull City, Alfreton Town
FACT SLOT: Ryan played in all four professional divisions during his time with Hull City.

16. ANDY TAYLOR
DoB: 14.3.86 , Accrington
Height: 6ft 0ins, Weight: 12st 6lbs
Signed from: Tranmere Rovers
Previous clubs: Tranmere Rovers, Huddersfield Town (loan), Crewe Alexandra (loan), Blackpool (loan), QPR (loan), Blackburn Rovers
FACT SLOT: Andy's nickname is Trigger, as some of his antics are like the character from Only Fools and Horses.

17. RICHARD CRESSWELL
DoB: 20.9.77 , Bridlington
Height: 6ft 1ins, Weight: 12st 13lbs
Signed from: Stoke City
Previous clubs: Stoke City, Leeds United, Preston North End, Leicester City, Sheffield Wednesday, Mansfield Town (loan), York City
FACT SLOT: Richard shares his name with an English politician who was born in 1688.

18. JAMIE WARD
DoB: 12.5.86, Birmingham
Height: 5ft 6ins, Weight: 10st 12lbs
Signed from: Chesterfield
Previous clubs: Chesterfield, Torquay United, Stockport County (loan), Aston Villa
FACT SLOT: One of Jamie's best friends in football is ex-Blades defender, Gary Cahill.

22. ROB KOZLUK
DoB: 5.8.77, Sutton-in-Ashfield
Height: 5ft 9ins, Weight: 11st 5lbs
Signed from: Barnsley
Previous clubs: Barnsley, Preston North End (loan), Wigan Athletic (loan), Huddersfield Town (loan), Sheffield United, Derby County
FACT SLOT: Despite re-signing in the summer, this is Rob's ninth season with the Blades!

23. KYLE BARTLEY
DoB: 22.5.91, Stockport
Height: 6ft 3ins, Weight: 14st 0lbs
Signed from: Arsenal (loan)
Previous clubs: Arsenal
FACT SLOT: Despite being an Arsenal player, Kyle is a known Manchester United fan.

28. STEPHEN QUINN
DoB: 4.4.86 , Dublin, Ireland
Height: 5ft 9ins, Weight: 11st 0lbs
Signed from: Youth team
Previous clubs: Rotherham United (loan), MK Dons (loan), St Patrick's Athletic
FACT SLOT: Three of Stephen's brothers have also played for United at differing levels.

34. MATTHEW LOWTON
DoB: 9.6.89, Chesterfield
Height: 5ft 11ins, Weight: 11st 9lbs
Signed from: Youth team
Previous clubs: Ferencvaros (loan)
FACT SLOT: Matt scored the winner in a pre-season friendly against Estudiantes in the summer.

DANIEL BOGDANOVIC

BLADES QUIZ

As 2011 approaches, it's an appropriate time to ask how much you remember about 2010? Here are ten questions from 2010 that will get you searching your brain for the answers...

1. Who scored United's first goal of 2010?
2. In which position did the Blades finish in the Championship last season?
3. How many games did Steve Simonsen play during his loan spell in March and April?
4. Who scored United's goal against Sheffield Wednesday at Hillsborough?
5. What number shirt was Mark Yeates handed when he signed in January?
6. For which club did Leon Britton play for against United in April?

7. Which Argentinean team did the Blades face in pre-season?
8. What nationality is Johnny Ertl?
9. In which two months in 2010 did the Blades play at Cardiff City's new stadium?
10. Who did United face in the first round of the Carling Cup in August?

27

RECORD BREAKERS

YOUNGEST

Steven Hawes was 17 years 47 days old when he became the youngest player to make a league appearance for the Blades, coming on as a substitute at West Brom on 2 September 1995. He made one League start and three sub appearances for United before moving to Doncaster Rovers and then Hull City. Steven has since moved into the non-leagues and his former clubs include Altrincham, Worksop Town, Stocksbridge Park Steels and Sheffield FC.

OLDEST

The oldest player to make a League appearance for United was Albert Sturgess. He joined the Blades from Stoke City in 1908 along with George Gallimore for the maximum transfer fee at the time of £350. A consistent and reliable player, Albert was primarily a left half, but he played in all outfield defensive positions. He gained an FA Cup winners medal in 1915 and won two England caps. He was 40 years and 124 days old when he played his last game for United in February 1923 but then moved to Norwich where he made 47 further appearances.

ALBERT STURGESS

TALLEST

At 6' 4" Greg Halford is one of United's tallest ever players. He had a successful season-long loan stint at the Lane in 2008-09 where he played in a variety of roles including twice as a striker, culminating in goals against Hull City in the FA Cup at Bramall Lane and a late equaliser against Plymouth Argyle at Home Park. Greg's renowned long-throw was utilised with great success by the Blades and his vital goal against Preston North End at the Lane in the second-leg of the play-off semi-final secured United's place at Wembley that campaign.

GREG HALFORD

SHORTEST

One of the smallest Blades is Alan Wright – recorded as being 5' 4". Having played at the top level for over 10 seasons, including being a member of Blackburn's Premiership winning team and a League Cup winner with Aston Villa, he joined United in October 2003. Alan's final appearance for United, after recovering from a cruciate ligament injury, was at the Emirates Stadium in the Premiership. In July 2009 he signed for Fleetwood Town and played a key role in their promotion to the Conference National last season.

ALAN WRIGHT

NICK MONTGOMERY

SPOT THE DIFFERENCE

Can you spot the SIX differences in the two images below?

TALKING GREAT GOALS

It is a great feeling to score for the Blades, but can you identify these scorers from what they said afterwards?

1. "When you score a goal like that it doesn't really register until you get home and see it on the television then it hits home what you have done – but it was my best goal by a mile."

2. "I'm happy to have scored, but disappointed with the injury. 'Morgs' headed it down and I just turned and hit it. It went in and I enjoyed the moment with the crowd. It is more special because of what was riding on the game."

3. "It took a big deflection, but I meant it – that's the only place where I could have put it! I think I showed a striker's instinct when the goalkeeper let the ball slip through his fingers."

4. "It is fantastic to come away with all three points. It was my first career hat-trick and I'm ecstatic at the minute. It was absolutely fantastic when the third one went in."

5. I had to make sure it was a good delivery as there wasn't long left so we needed something from a set-piece. 'Cressy' tried to claim it, along with 'Morgs' and Ched, but I can confirm it is my goal."

6. "Andy Taylor put a great ball in for me to get on the end of and I managed to stoop low and force it home. You have got to be brave in those situations and fortunately the ball squirmed over the line."

7. "It was a bit unreal. I managed to control the ball on my thigh, swivel and volley it home. It was a pleasure to see it hit the back of the net because it is such a long time since my last goal."

8. "I remember Dion Dublin doing something similar a long time ago. I just had a feeling that he was going to put the ball down, and when he did I managed to get in front of him and slide it in."

9. "It has been a long time coming. Henri pulled it back and I stepped onto the ball and managed to power it in. I think there was a slight deflection but the goalkeeper wouldn't have got to it anyway, he didn't move."

10. "I knew the amount of pressure there was on the game and what it meant to the fans, so it is nice to get the goal that earned us a point. In training we speak about the amount of free-kicks that you see go in at the far post. The Gaffer tells us to aim for there and that's what I did – luckily it went in."

STRIKING

SHEFFIELD UNITED F.C.
1889

TOP 10 TIPS

Scoring goals isn't as easy as it looks from the stands, so here are some useful tips on becoming the next Ched Evans.

1. Work hard – Play your heart out from the first whistle to the last, because you never know when you might get that chance to score that all important goal.

2. Be a team player – The object is for the team to score, not the individual. If someone else has a better chance than you, pass the ball to them.

3. Accuracy is as important as power – No matter how hard you can hit the ball, to have a chance of scoring it must be on target.

4. Follow through – Strike the ball with your laces and don't stop your leg motion once you have connected with the ball. If you swing your leg through it will give you more momentum.

5. Aim for the corners – They are the hardest places for the goalkeeper to protect.

6. Practice makes perfect – Practice shooting at a small target to improve your accuracy. In time you can gradually increase your distance from the object, so you can soon be scoring some spectacular goals.

7. Attack...attack...attack – Make the defenders and goalkeeper work hard because the more shots you have the more likely you are to score.

8. Be patient – Don't panic if the ball isn't coming because a chance could come at anytime.

9. Be able to play with both feet – This will come through practice and in time you will be a good all-round player. The more skills you have, the more chance you have got of getting past defenders.

10. Be confident – If you get a chance, take it! If you think you can beat your defender, go for it! Make your decision and be decisive to try and out-fox the defender.

CHED EVANS

33

GOALKEEPING

TOP 10 TIPS

Being a goalkeeper is a tough job, so if you think you are man enough to follow Steve into United's number one shirt, here are some top tips from United's No.1 to get you on track.

STEVE SIMONSEN

1. Stay on your toes – As a goalkeeper your feet should be constantly moving, so you are ready for anything that is coming your way. Never stand on your heels, that's when you might get caught out and make a mistake.

2. Shout...Loud! – You have to communicate with your team-mates, especially your defenders, let them know what you are doing early to avoid confusion. A nice, early decision from you will make their life easier too.

3. Stay relaxed – If you are tense and nervous, diving and getting hit with the ball will hurt more!

4. Stay awake – You have got to be watching the game from start to finish, to make sure you are ready when it is your chance to shine. Remember, a game can change completely in a matter of seconds.

5. Watch players' feet – The way the attacker's feet are positioned when he is going to kick the ball can indicate where it might be going.

6. Bounce back – After diving to make a save, recover quickly, because the game doesn't stop because you are on the floor.

7. Stay square to the ball – At all times, keep your hips and shoulders pointing at the shooter.

8. Never take a save for granted – No matter how weak the shot is or how easy the save looks, always make sure you get the ball under full control. If you are lazy then you might make a silly mistake.

9. Get your body behind the ball – That way if the ball slips through your fingers, your body will be there to stop it.

10. Be proud – Take pride in your position as you are the last line of defence for your team. You must have confidence in yourself and be prepared to put your body in positions where you may get hurt, but that save could win the match.

DEFENDING

TOP 10 TIPS

The United skipper is regarded as one of the best defenders in the Championship and strikers know they will be in for a hard time against him. Here is his advice to get you following in his footsteps.

CHRIS MORGAN

1. Apply pressure – It is important your opponent knows you are there and often that can force them into a mistake. If you can make things tough for them then they are less likely to score a goal.

2. Mark your man – You always need to know where your attacker is, never let him get in behind you or you'll lose sight of the ball.

3. Be on the ball – Stay alert, keep your concentration and be on your toes so you are ready to sprint after a loose ball.

4. Keep your eyes on the ball – Don't let the ball out of your sight, that way you shouldn't get caught out of position.

5. Listen to your goalkeeper – He often has a better view of what is going on around the pitch and he will be able to help you.

6. Don't make rash tackles – If you don't think you can win the ball cleanly, then don't dive in or make a slide tackle, because you are more likely to be penalised.

7. Never think you are beaten – If an attacker beats you, chase back and attempt to put some pressure on him.

8. Be tough – Tackle hard, but always go for the ball, not the man.

9. Watch the game – Be aware of what is happening and watch for passes that you can intercept.

10. Work as a team – If a fellow defender is tracking the attacker, be there to cover him. You must act as the next line of defence so the opposition doesn't get a clear view of the goal.

AND THE WINNER IS
...MAINLY MONTY!

End of season Player of the Year award ceremonies are something that footballers enjoy. We are not just talking about professionals as the United lads, like thousands of others, would have been to plenty of presentation nights as they grew up. However, it does not matter if you have been to 3 or 3,000 award ceremonies, the players will still tell you that they get the same buzz when the main award of the night – usually Player of the Year is preceded by the phrase... 'and the winner is...'

Here's a few of United's winners from the end of last season.

Nick Montgomery receives the Malta Tourism Authority's Player of the Year Trophy

Nick Montgomery and Richard Cresswell are named joint winners of the GAC Logistics Players' Player of the Year award

Jamie Ward and Chris Morgan share the East Midlands Trains Community Player of the Year.

The Halliwells Goal of the Season goes to Richard Cresswell for his 'cheeky' finish against Plymouth Argyle

Nick Montgomery also picks up the Sheffield United Player of the Year title at The Star and Green 'Un football awards.

Chris Morgan is crowned the Official Supporters' Club Player of the Year.

The runner up in the Official Supporters' Club Player of the Year is Jamie Ward.

LANE LEGENDS

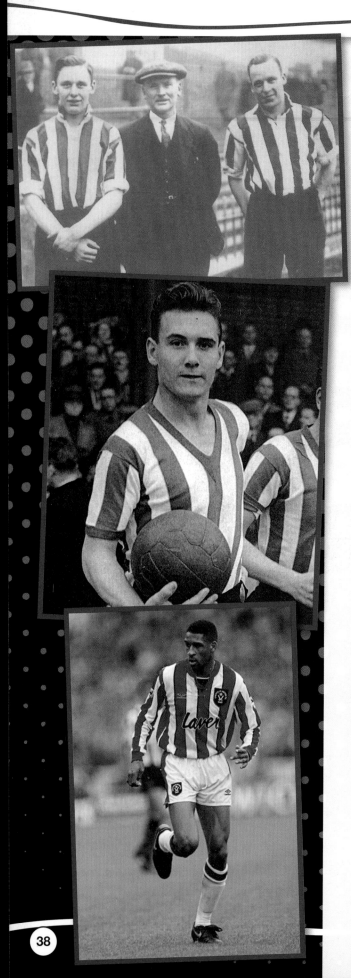

HARRY JOHNSON

Between 1919 and 1931 Harry scored 201 league goals for the Blades and 20 more in the FA Cup – more than any other player. Harry once scored five goals in a game against West Ham United, whilst he managed four goals in a game seven times and netted twelve hat-tricks.
His father (also Harry) and his brother Tom also played for United making the Johnsons a real Blades family.

JOE SHAW

Joe Shaw made 632 league appearances for the Blades between 1948 and 1966 – more than any other player and a statue of him was unveiled in the car park at the Lane in August. Joe started his career as an inside forward then moved to wing half before establishing himself at centre half. Although only 5' 8" tall he read the game fantastically well and many in the game, not just in Sheffield, felt he should have played for England.

BRIAN DEANE

Signed for £40,000 from Doncaster Rovers in the close season of 1988, Brian formed a deadly partnership with Tony Agana as United gained promotion from the old Division 3. The following season he spearheaded the charge to the top-flight, scoring 21 league goals as United secured consecutive promotions. In 1992, Brian netted the first ever Premier League goal as the Blades beat Manchester United 2-1 at Bramall Lane. The popular striker also won three England caps during his first of three stints with the club.

TONY CURRIE

After arriving at the Lane from Watford in February 1968, Tony scored on his debut and delighted Unitedites for the following eight seasons. Renowned for his tremendous ball control, passing and dribbling skills, TC also had a physical strength that added more to his all-round game. His great vision and distribution won him seven England caps with United and 17 in total. Arguably his most famous goal was described on Match of the Day as 'a quality goal by a quality player'.

JIMMY HAGAN

Jimmy was perhaps United's greatest player of all-time. He joined the Blades in 1938 from Derby County and scored a hat-trick in the final game of that season that clinched promotion to the top-flight - at the expense of Sheffield Wednesday. The Second World War saw Jimmy miss seven seasons and although his scoring record was respectable, it was his technical skill and speed of thought which wowed the Bramall Lane faithful, leaving it a mystery how he only won one England cap.

ERNEST 'NUDGER' NEEDHAM

'Nudger' joined United in 1891, played in the Club's first ever League game and was a fixture in the side for over 17 years. He was United's captain when they were League Champions in 1898 and FA Cup winners (1899 and 1902). Although small, 'Nudger' was known by those he played with as 'the Prince of half backs'. He played for England 16 times and was the first professional player to captain England, whilst he also played county cricket for Derbyshire.

JOHNNY ERTL

SPOT THE BALL

SHEFFIELD UNITED F.C.
1889

Can you use your skills to spot the ball in the picture below?

Answer page 60

10 THINGS ABOUT
THE BLADES

1 Only two United players have scored for the club at Wembley – Fred Tunstall netted the winning goal against Cardiff City in the 1925 FA Cup Final and Alan Cork scored against Sheffield Wednesday in the 1993 FA Cup Semi-Final.

When the Blades beat Arsenal 6-2 in 1920-21 they became the only club to score six goals against Arsenal at Highbury in a competitive fixture.

2

3

4 At Burnley in 2003, two goalkeepers made their debuts for the Blades. Lee Baxter played in the first half and conceded three goals. At half time he was replaced by Alan Fettis, who kept a clean sheet.

The first ever football match played at Bramall Lane, which was a very different looking ground in those days, was one between Sheffield FC and Hallam. It was played on 29 December 1862 and ended in a goalless draw.

5

In the 1969-70 season, United beat Portsmouth 5-1 at Fratton Park and 5-0 at Bramall Lane. In the first meeting the following season, at Portsmouth, the Blades scored five again, winning 5-1. Alan Woodward scored five goals in total, finding the net in each game.

6

Many pairs of brothers have played for United, but the ones who played most often together were Barry and Tony Wagstaff. They appeared together in 51 league games for the Blades.

7

The famous Newcastle and England centre forward Jackie Milburn, or 'Wor Jackie' as he was known, played one game for the Blades. He was a guest player for a Second World War game at Hillsborough in May 1945. Sadly United lost 2-4.

8

In his first four games for United against our city rivals Wednesday, Alan Birchenall netted six of the seven goals scored by the Blades. United won two and drew one of the four games.

9

Carl Muggleton had one of the shortest careers with the Blades. As a goalkeeper he was on the bench on several occasions but made just one substitute appearance, coming on for about two minutes at the end of the game at Reading in April 1996. What made his appearance unusual was that he came on as an outfield substitute – but never touched the ball!

10

Since the Second World War only three United players have scored four goals in a competitive game for the Blades. Derek Pace and Alan Woodward managed it once but Keith Edwards did so twice, both times in the 1983-84 season, against Gillingham in the League and at Wrexham in the FA Cup.

WORDSEARCH

Take a look through the letters below to find
the names of these 12 Blades captains

```
Q G G S I N G D W J W T X D T
F L E W A K O A H Z H V S B T
O H J S S P D Y B G J B H Q L
O V D D H I D C I P C X P W Z
E U H M A K I E M Y K H I U S
K H R S W Y P Q G A A O E N H
Z Q O N T S E U I N V L D T Q
C C O U G A H P A H Y P R B K
R O E P S Z N G Z A H O Y H H
Y L J J F T R C G H W B Y T A
T D N P E O O T L S M E R J G
Y W K Z M U H N D I L N I O A
Y E P A G E T L E T F B B N N
V L L Y Q B O I U D V F L E P
M L J D A H A T K L D R E S Q
```

HAGAN
PAGE
STANCLIFFE
JONES
COLDWELL
SPEIGHT
SHAW
UTLEY
GAYLE
MORGAN
HOLDSWORTH
HOUSTON

WARPED FACES

Can you work out who these two players are?
A clue is that they are both summer signings.

Answer page 60

44

STEPHEN QUINN

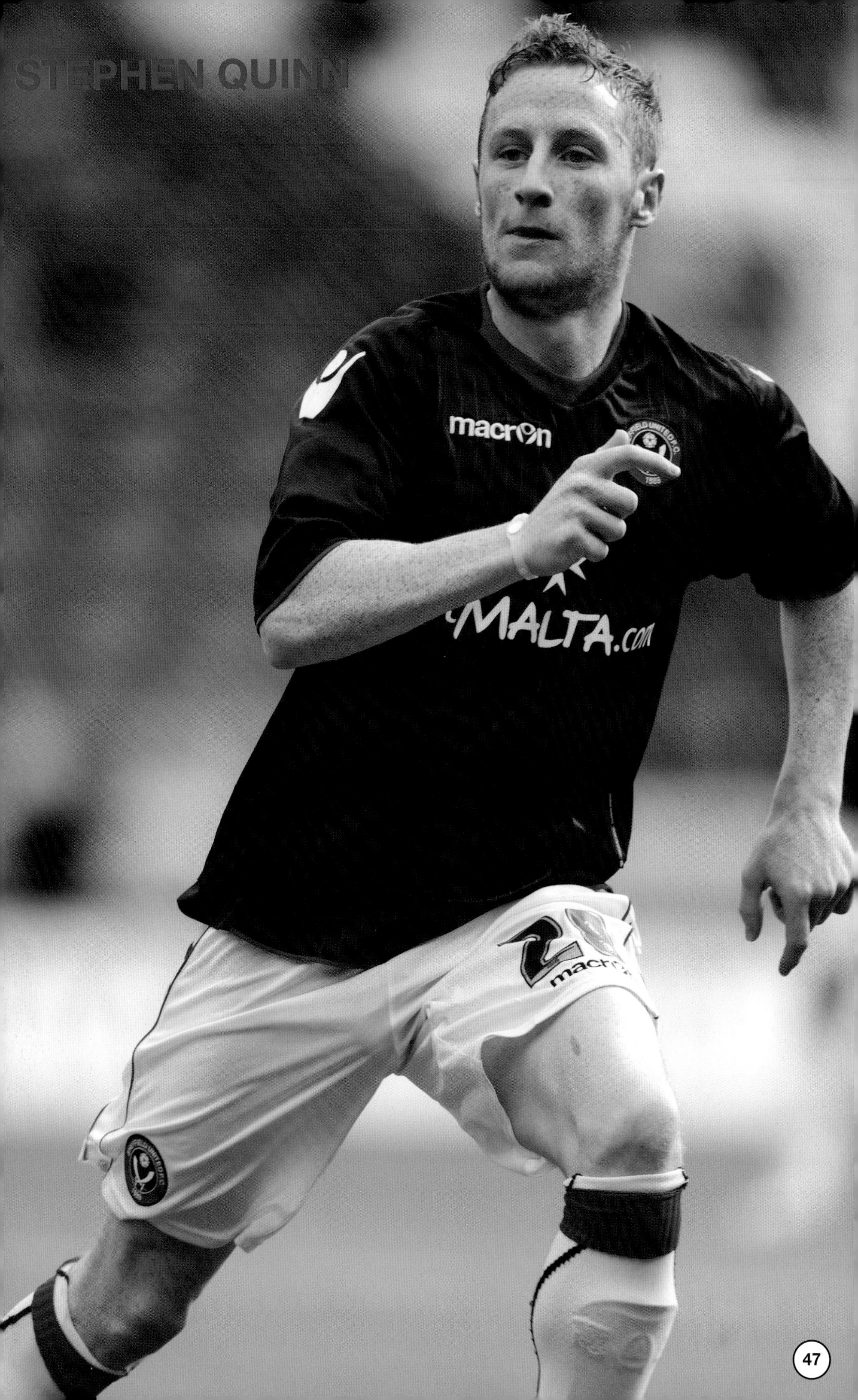

AYE AYE CAPTAIN!

Captain Blade is a must-see at Bramall Lane on matchday, along with his mate, Mister Cutler, and you will always see him dancing, celebrating or – if he gets the chance - generally making a nuisance of himself or cheating at everything!

But he doesn't just turn up for matches, he also gets involved in other events, sometimes with mascots from other teams when they have races or competitions, or at charity events so you never quite know where he will pop up next, as you can see from our pictures from last season.

Of course, he is now wearing his special shirt for the current 2010-11 season and it is specially made to fit his captain's uniform.

We think he is one of the smartest and most recognisable club mascots around and he is always glad to see our supporters, so give him a wave when he passes you at the Lane.

To find out if Captain Blade is available for your charity event, call the Commercial Department on 0871 663 2462

BLADES EXPERT

Want to make yourself a Blades Expert? Find out on these pages the main things to know about Sheffield United – and keep looking out for more information to boost your knowledge about the club.

The Blades have been League Champions just once in 1898, but this was only nine years after the club was formed. No other club has become the best in the country so quickly. United played two challenge matches against Celtic, the Scottish League champions drawing one and winning the other. United were therefore the unofficial 'Champions of Great Britain'

Plaque marks the spot

United were formed on 22 March 1889. Following a successful FA Cup semi-final at Bramall Lane it was decided, at a meeting at 10 Norfolk Row, to form a football club to play regularly at Bramall Lane, to provide money in the winter. Previously it had been used primarily for cricket with just special football games being played at the ground.

Cup Finals

United have won the FA Cup four times in 1899, 1902, 1915 and 1925. They also reached the final in 1901 and 1936. In 1901 they lost to Tottenham Hotspur, then in the Southern League, who were the last club outside the Football League or Premiership to win the famous cup. Bramall Lane was the venue for an FA Cup Final. Barnsley beat West Bromwich Albion 1-0 in a replayed final in 1912.

Blades brothers in arms

When United won the FA Cup in 1925 young Harry Johnson and Thomas

Boyle gained medals. Their fathers 'old Harry Johnson' and Peter Boyle had both won FA Cup winners medals with United in 1899 and 1902. 'Young Harry's' brother Tom also played for United in the 1936 Cup Final defeat to Arsenal.

United joined the Football league in 1892 in the newly formed Second Division. Promotion and relegation was decided by Test Matches (similar to the modern Play offs). United beat Accrington and were promoted and so became, along with Darwen (who beat Notts County), one of the first two clubs to be promoted.

Bramall Lane

Of the League grounds still in use, only five were used for Football League games before Bramall Lane: Anfield, Deepdale, Turf Moor, Molineux and Ewood Park. The world's first ever floodlit football match was held at Bramall Lane in October 1878. The lights were portable ones powered by generators and the two teams were each captained by one of the Clegg brothers. The first England vs Scotland match outside London or Glasgow was played at Bramall Lane on 10 March 1883. Scotland won 3-2.

Bombs on the pitch!

Due to bomb damage at Bramall Lane in December 1940 United had to play some of their 'home' matches elsewhere. Five were played at Hillsborough and one at Millmoor.

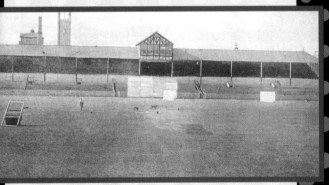

Deano first off the mark

At the start of the 1992-93 season United were founder members of the newly formed Premier League. Brian Deane scored the first ever Premier League goal and the first ever Premier League penalty as United beat Manchester United 2-1.

In the early days of Sheffield football the press referred to both United and Wednesday as 'The Blades', but the nickname was eventually used just for United.

Ground of stars

Bramall Lane staged an Ashes Test Match in July 1902. United's home, along with The Oval, are the only two grounds to stage a Test Match, an FA Cup Final and an international football match.

Owls pipped

At the end of the 1938-39 season United had to win their final match of the season at home against Spurs to gain promotion to the top flight. If they failed Sheffield Wednesday would be promoted. United won 6-1 and pipped the Owls by one point.

CELEBRATION TIME!

Jamie Ward is jubilant after scoring United's second in the 3-1 success at Reading, their first away win of the season.

The 'pocket-rocket' fired home the opener as the Blades scored three in the first-half against Sheffield Wednesday at Bramall Lane in September, a game they eventually won 3-2.

Darius Henderson holds the captain's armband aloft following one of his penalties at Oakwell, as a sign of unity to skipper Chris Morgan, who missed the game at Oakwell through suspension.

Stephen Quinn congratulates Richard Cresswell, after his goal against Reading put United 2-0 up before half-time.

'Morgs' gets the final touch to Jamie Ward's goal-bound header, with the helpless Adam Federici looking on, as the Blades make it three against the Royals.

The team celebrate Lee Williamson's spectacular equaliser in front of the Kop at Hillsborough in April.

JAMIE WARD
TALKING

JAMIE'S OPINIONS

Best player in the world...
"It's got to be Lionel Messi, he proves small is best"

Best English player...
"For his goals last season, I'd say Wayne Rooney"

Best friend in football...
"Two from my Villa days, Gary Cahill and Craig Gardner"

United's dressing room joker...
"Myself and Rob Kozluk – and now we room together on away trips!"

Advice to young players...
"Work hard and don't let people knock your confidence"

JAMIE'S FAVOURITES

Football memory...
"Scoring against Sheffield Wednesday last season"

Holiday destination...
"It's got to be Dubai, a fantastic place"

Football team...
"Aston Villa – I supported them before I went there at the age of eight"

Other sport...
"Boxing, I like to watch the big fights on TV"

Pastime...
"Laying on the sofa, watching the TV – I can do that for hours"

JAMIE WARD
HAS PLENTY TO SAY...

TRUE COLOURS

Can you finish this picture of Andy Taylor and colour it in?

ANDY TAYLOR

NUMBERS GAME

Can you do these sums by using players' squad numbers? For instance Daniel Bogdanovic is number 10 and Leon Britton is number 8. Add them together and you get Jamie Ward who is number 18. Can you do the others?

 +  =

1. Daniel Bogdanovic + Leon Britton = Jamie Ward

2. Steve Simonsen + Stephen Jordan =

3. Darius Henderson – Nyron Nosworthy =

4. Daniel Bogdanovic + Ched Evans - Jamie Ward =

5. Johnny Ertl + Mark Yeates =

6. Chris Morgan + Ched Evans =

7. Chris Morgan x Nyron Nosworthy =

8. Ryan France + Mihkel Aksalu =

9. Stephen Quinn - Kyle Bartley + Nyron Nosworthy =

10. Matt Lowton - Rob Kozluk + Darius Henderson - Lee Williamson =

SQUAD NUMBERS

1 Steve Simonsen, 2 Stephen Jordan, 3 Nyron Nosworthy, 4 Nick Montgomery, 5 Chris Morgan, 6 Johnny Ertl, 7 Darius Henderson, 8 Leon Britton, 9 Ched Evans, 10 Daniel Bogdanovic, 11 Mark Yeates, 13 Mihkel Aksalu, 14 Lee Williamson, 15 Ryan France, 16 Andy Taylor, 17 Richard Cresswell, 18 Jamie Ward, 22 Rob Kozluk, 23 Kyle Bartley, 28 Stephen Quinn, 30 Kingsley James, 31 Jordan Chapell, 32 Phil Roe, 34 Matthew Lowton

Answer page 61

MARK YEATES

NAME THE STADIUM

Can you name these grounds?
Six English football stadiums are pictured below…
How many do you recognise?

Answer page 61

LEON OF THE LANE

How much do you know about little Britton?

- In 1998, Leon was the subject of the highest ever transfer fee paid for a 16-year-old when he moved from Arsenal to West Ham.

- Leon scored a penalty for Swansea when he played against United at Bramall Lane in the FA Cup back in 2007.

- In 2003, Leon was named the Third Division's PFA Player of the Year – the only Swansea player to ever win the award.

- At around 163cm high (about 5ft 4ins), Leon is the smallest player in United's first team squad.

- In seven and a half years at Swansea, Leon made over 300 appearances for the Welsh side, helping them to two promotions.

QUIZ ANSWERS

Blades Quiz page 27

1. Richard Cresswell
2. Eighth
3. Seven
4. Lee Williamson
5. Eleven
6. Swansea City
7. Estudiantes
8. Austrian
9. March and August
10. Hartlepool United

Spot the Ball page 41

Spot the Difference page 31

Talking Great Goals page 32

1. Keith Treacy v Leicester City
   Jamie Ward v Sheffield Wednesday
3. Chris Morgan v Ipswich Town
4. Darius Henderson at Bristol City
5. Jamie Ward v Preston North End
6. Richard Cresswell v Middlesbrough
7. Jonathan Fortune v Reading
8. Richard Cresswell v Plymouth Argyle
9. Nick Montgomery vt Blackpool
10. Lee Williamson at Sheffield Wednesday

Wordsearch and Warped Faces page 44

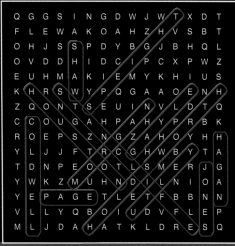

A. Britton

B. Bogdanovic

Stars in their Eyes page 46

1. Johnny Ertl
2. Richard Creswell
3. Rob Kozluk
4. Stephen Quinn
5. Nick Montgomery
6. Leon Britton
7. Chris Morgan
8. Mark Yeates

Number Game page 56

1. Jamie Ward
2. Nyron Nosworthy
3. Nick Montgomery
4. Steve Simonsen
5. Richard Cresswell
6. Lee Williamson
7. Ryan France
8. Stephen Quinn
9. Leon Britton
10. Chris Morgan

Name the Stadium page 58

1. Anfield

2. Goodison Park

3. Old Trafford

5. Wembley

4. St James' Park

6. Upton Park

WE'RE ALL BLADES AREN'T WE?